THE ADVENTURES OF ME AND DAD

THE ADVENTURES OF ME AND DAD

THE SPACE ADVENTURE

JOHN BONIFANT

Johnbonifant

Dedicated to my Son.

"hey Dad, can you tell me a bedtime story?" "Sure buddy,
what kind?" "I...I want an adventure story." "Alright, buddy."
"How about a space adventure story?" "ooo that sounds like a
good one."
"There once was a man that loved adventure. The man would
go on these crazy, cool adventures and when he would return
home he would tell his son all about them. One story, in
particular, was about his voyage across the stars, how he would
fly across the galaxy and look at all the magic and splendor that
it held. There are so many amazing things out here that he just
had to bring his son with him on his next trip. This is their story.

"Hey buddy, wake up. I'm home. Guess what?" "What Dad?"
his son replied. "Would you like to come with me on my next trip
through the stars?" "Yes!" Shouted his son. "Well, let's go then, Go
get your shoes on and make it fast because there is a lot to see,
And we only have a little bit of time before Mom has dinner ready."
He threw his shoes on in haste, turned, looked at his
dad, and said "Do I need a jacket?" "Yes!" said his father. "It gets
kind of chilly up there." So Tommy ran and grabbed his coat.
"Meet me in the backyard," said Dad. So, as Tommy waited for
his dad to arrive, he started getting excited about what he
would see once they flew to the stars. "Hey buddy, come here, I
need some help." Shouted Dad. so Tommy ran over to his dad,
With a confused look on his face, he said to his dad, "Why
do you have all of those boxes for?" "Well, we have to build a
Rocketship out of them before we can fly to the stars." So, there
in the backyard, Tommy helped his dad build a rocket ship out of
all the boxes his dad had brought, and when they were done it
was the most magical, most awesome thing Tommy had seen
. "Get in Tommy." Said dad. "We need to get this thing up
to the stars." As Tommy sat inside the Rocketship his dad told
him to hold on tight because they were getting ready for takeoff.
"Tommy, do you want to start the countdown? Start at 10" said
Dad. "Ok, said Tommy." "10,9,8."(at the count of 8 he felt the
spaceship start to rumble.) "7,6,5....4....3....2.....1." As soon as
Tommy said one, He felt this sudden jolt of power shoot the
Rocketship straight up off the ground.

When Tommy looked through the window that was next to him, He could see the Earth, He could see the ocean, He could see all the land, He could even see all the tiny lights that covered the land. "Dad what are all those lights from?" said Tommy, "Well those are all the people, all those lights tell you where people live." said Dad. But as he was watching the Earth, He didn't realize that it was getting smaller and smaller.

Then all of a sudden, This big gray and white object started to move past his window. That's when his dad leaned in and said, "That's the moon." Tommy looked in awe as the moon passed. " The universe is full of so much amazing wonder" Said Tommy. "What would you like to do first? What would you like to see?" Dad asked. "I want to see it all." Said Tommy. "Awesome!" said Dad. "Well the first stop will be the sun," said Dad. As the Rocketship turned away from the moon Tommy could see this big, bright, yellowish, and orange light. So massive that it filled the whole window. "Feel that?" Dad asked. "what?" questioned Tommy. "Do you feel how hot it is getting in here?" Dad asked. "Yes!" Exclaimed Tommy. "All the heat and light that we get on earth comes from the sun, What makes the sun so amazing is that even though it is so far away, we can still see its light and feel its warmth. The sun is what helps the Plants, Trees, and Animals grow. It gives us the hope that tomorrow will always be bright and filled with wonder and warmth." Dad said. "Amazing, isn't it Tommy." "It is so amazing!" said Tommy.

"There are also two little planets that are between the Sun and the Earth. The one closest to the sun is called Mercury, The second one is Venus. Mercury is smaller than Venus, But unlike Earth, No one lives there." Dad said. "Why?" asked Tommy. "Because it is too hot, And none of them have oxygen like Earth does.

Every living thing needs oxygen to live," said Dad. "If you look out that window you will be able to see both planets." Dad said. "see them?" Dad exclaimed. "Yes, I do, right there, and you're right, Mercury is the smallest of the two planets," said Tommy.

"Now let's fly over to Mars, the red planet," Dad said. "Is
that the one by Earth?" asked Tommy. "yes" Dad said. "Tommy,
look out your window, You can now see Mars," Dad said. As
Tommy looked through his window he could see this red-colored
the planet moves across his window. "Dad, why do they call Mars the
red planet?" asked Tommy. "Because of the dirt that is on the
surface of Mars. When you look at the dirt it looks red, because
of all the iron in the dirt." Dad said. "Oh, I see now," said Tommy.
"Now let's go to the biggest planet in our Solar System, Jupiter."
said Dad.

As the Rocketship moved away from Mars Tommy's dad turned to him and said "Now that we are passing Mars, We need to watch out for Asteroids. See those small and big rocks floating around over there. This is a whole group of them that floats between Mars and Jupiter, In a big circle called the Asteroid Belt. The Sun, Mercury, Venus, Earth, Moon, and Mars are in the center of the Asteroid Belt, With Jupiter, Saturn, Uranus, Neptune, and even a tiny Darf planet called Pluto, Being on the outside of the Asteroid Belt." Exclaimed Dad. "Wow," said Tommy. "Are those big rocks heavy?" Tommy asked. "Yes, some of them weigh thousands upon thousands of pounds, and some of them weigh even more than that," Dad answered.

As Tommy smiled, he thought to himself. "This is the best day of my life!" As Tommy was looking out of his window into the vast, endless, open space called Outer Space, he saw a huge planet move in front of his window. Tommy thought "Wow, that's huge!" He didn't realize that they still weren't close enough to see the full scope of the planet. But then he noticed the big red circle that was floating on the planet. It looked like somebody had just finished mixing strawberry and vanilla ice cream.

"Dad, what is that giant red spot on Jupiter?" asked Tommy. "Well," said Dad. "That spot is where all the angry storms are located," "Like the Thunder and Lightning!" Added Tommy. "yes, but this storm is a million times worse than what we have ever seen. It is so bad there that if the same storm was on Earth it would destroy everything." Dad said sadly.

"Well let's move on to Saturn, one of my favorite planets!" Dad said excitedly. As they moved away from Jupiter, The most amazing sight came into view. It was a huge planet, Not as huge as Jupiter but still pretty big. As it moved into sight. "Dad is that Saturn?" "Yes son, it is" "Wow, that's amazing! Look at all those colors, Are those rings around it?" Tommy asked. "Yes, Tommy those are rings. And yes, just look at all those colors. Saturn is an amazing planet." "Here bud, put this space suit on. Let's go take a walk." As Tommy was putting on his suit, he looked over to his dad and saw that his dad was doing the same thing. Once Tommy and his dad had both put on their suits, the The rocketship's hatch was opened. "Come on Tommy," said his dad, "Let's go touch the rings." As Tommy got out of the Rocketship, he was able to float over to the rings and run his fingers through them. Tommy was not able to explain the feeling he had when he saw how the dust from the rings just floated away, Tommy realized how they felt cold just like ice. At that moment Tommy looked back around to the Rocketship to see his dad waving at him, "come on Tommy, we need to head over to Uranus,"

As Tommy boarded the Rocketship and took off his
suit, his dad picked him up, sat him down on the seat, and
buckled him in. His dad turned towards the front, grabbed
the controls, looked over at Tommy, and said. "push the go
button." So Tommy did, and with a sudden rush of power, the
Rocketship shot off to Uranus. Tommy watched as the big blue
planet came into view. He also noticed that it was a lot colder
than it was before. "Dad, it is getting colder," Tommy said. "Yes,
it is," said his dad. "the further you get away from the sun the
colder it gets. Plus, Uranus is nicknamed the icy giant because
it is mostly ice, and it is very cold on that planet," said Dad. As
they made a pass around Uranus Tommy asked, "Is that why it's
blue?" "Yes, Because of all the cold elements that the planet is
made out of. Now let's move on to Neptune." Dad said.

As Neptune moved into view, Tommy realized that it looked somewhat the same as Jupiter. That's when his dad chimed in and spoke. "Neptune is the smallest gas giant in our Solar System. It is also named after the Roman God of the sea because it looks like it is completely covered in water, which makes it look like a vast ocean." Tommy had no words because he was just so mesmerized by the sight of the planet.

Next stop is Pluto," Dad said. "You know Tommy, when I was growing up, Pluto was a planet, but now it's called a Dwarf planet. It is also named after the Roman God of the underworld." "Dad why is it called a Dwarf planet," Tommy asked. "Because the planet is tiny," answered Dad. "But why did they name it after the God of the underworld," Tommy questioned. "Because when you look at Pluto the planet is very barren and dark, nothing can grow here, just like what you may see in the underworld." answered Dad. As they circled Pluto, Tommy just could not stop staring at the barren, dark planet."

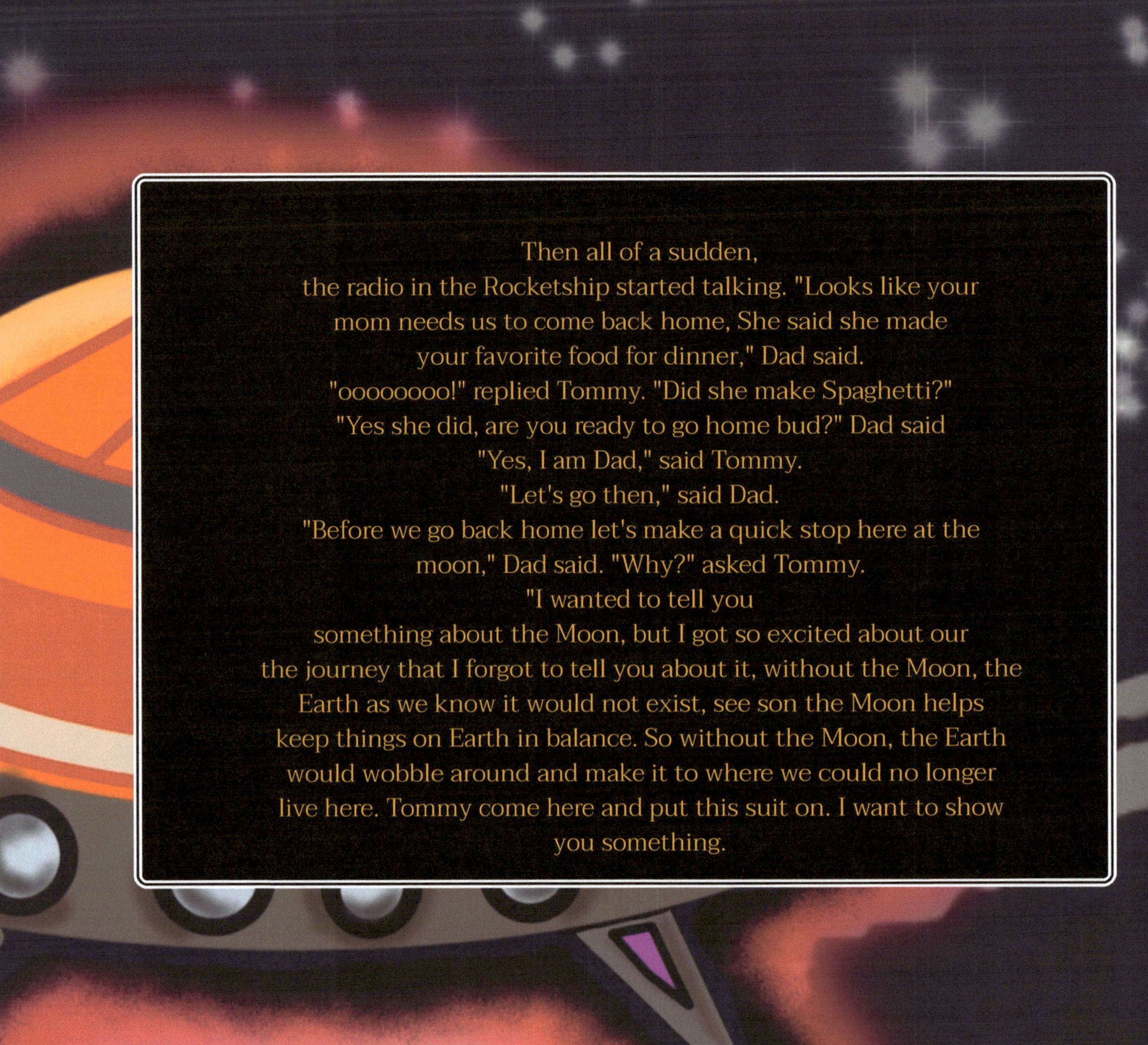

Then all of a sudden,
the radio in the Rocketship started talking. "Looks like your
mom needs us to come back home, She said she made
your favorite food for dinner," Dad said.
"oooooooo!" replied Tommy. "Did she make Spaghetti?"
"Yes she did, are you ready to go home bud?" Dad said
"Yes, I am Dad," said Tommy.
"Let's go then," said Dad.
"Before we go back home let's make a quick stop here at the
moon," Dad said. "Why?" asked Tommy.
"I wanted to tell you
something about the Moon, but I got so excited about our
the journey that I forgot to tell you about it, without the Moon, the
Earth as we know it would not exist, see son the Moon helps
keep things on Earth in balance. So without the Moon, the Earth
would wobble around and make it to where we could no longer
live here. Tommy come here and put this suit on. I want to show
you something.

The reason I wanted to bring you on this
adventure with me is to show you just how magnificent and
awesome Outer space is. Look around, what do you see?" Dad
asked "Well,... I see a lot of empty space." Tommy said. "It's
only empty because we have not explored it yet." Explained
Dad.
"Now my son, let's get you home." said dad
"Dad thank you," said Tommy. "For what buddy?" asked Dad.
"For taking me out on this trip. It was the best day of my life!"
exclaimed Tommy. "Well buddy, there will be plenty more, I
promise". said Dad.

"Time for bed buddy, Good night, I love you," Dad said.
"Love you to Dad, That was a great story," Tommy said happily.

Imagination is a key factor in a child's development, without it,
they can't create imaginary dreams that could, in the future take
them to the stars and beyond. without it, they can't create hopes
or dreams.

Thanks for reading this book.